Stop Smoking w

BY THE SAME AUTHOR
Stop Smoking: Real Help at Last
Smoking is a Psychological Problem
Midlife: Problems and Solutions (Editor)

Stop Smoking with the Symonds Method

Dr Gabriel Symonds

All you need to know to stop smoking easily

YOUCAXTON PUBLICATIONS
OXFORD AND SHREWSBURY

The painting 'Nicotine Monkey on the Back' by Don Ivan Punchatz is reproduced with kind permission of Gregor Punchatz.

Acknowledgement: Roger Brookin, for many stimulating discussions.

ISBN 978-1-912419-55-5

Printed and bound in Great Britain.
Published by YouCaxton Publications 2018
www.youcaxton.co.uk

Contents

Introduction

The Symonds Method

Appendix:
Conventional Ways to Quit Smoking

Introduction

First encounter with the smoking problem

This is a photo is of me aged about two on Primrose Hill in north London with a friend of my father's and his daughter. It was shortly after the end of the Second World War.

It was considered normal to smoke in those days, although I appear to be looking disapprovingly at him even at that tender age!

This unfortunate man one day suddenly coughed up some blood. He was diagnosed with lung cancer and stopped smoking immediately. The diseased part of his lung was removed and he was lucky to survive in reasonable health for the next twenty years.

Early attempts to help smokers quit

As a general practitioner (family doctor) I would regularly come across patients who were suffering from smoking-related diseases. The problem, of course, was how to get them to stop.

I found it upsetting to see people damaging their health by the – as it seemed to me – pointless, unnecessary and self-imposed activity of smoking and by my inability to do much about it for them.

Telling smokers of the risks they were running – and as I doctor I knew what I was talking about – even for those who said they wanted to quit, had little effect.

Another way I tried was to advise them that when they felt they the need to smoke they should wait five minutes, timed by the clock. Then wait another five minutes. And another. And eventually the urge to smoke, the 'craving', would go away.

This wasn't notable for its success either.

Many of these patients were intelligent, educated people. Why did it seem so difficult, even for them, to stop smoking?

I didn't really know but I was determined to find out.

Listening to smokers

It soon became clear to me that scientific studies about brain function, neurochemistry and addiction, though interesting in themselves, were not of the slightest help in a practical sense.

So I started talking to my smoker patients and listening to what they said. This was a rich source of information that I couldn't find in any medical book or journal.

In fact, *everything I now know about smoking I learnt from my patients.*

Unlike the usual kind of research where people are questioned using box-ticking methods, I asked open-ended questions such as these:

- *Why do you smoke?*
- *What does it do for you?*
- *What do you get out of it?*
- *What happens when you don't smoke?*
- *What do you actually feel when you want a cigarette but can't smoke for one reason or another?*

The answers, or sometimes the lack of an answer, were revealing.

Based on what hundreds of my smoker patients told me I gradually developed a method of quitting smoking that I found worked in nearly every case.

I call it the Symonds Method.

The Symonds Method

Is easy quitting possible?

It's my intention to show you how you truly can stop smoking easily – without nicotine, drugs, hypnosis or gimmicks of any kind. Even willpower is not required.

This may seem a bold claim but, based on my experience, *almost everything most people believe about smoking is wrong.*

How can this be?

Surely, the experts at the local stop-smoking services must know what they're talking about! After all, they use what are called evidence-based treatments, don't they?

This sounds hopeful, but with the methods in common use, such as nicotine patches or gum or prescription drugs, the results of scientific studies show that at best only 20% of smokers who accept this kind of help are not smoking one year later – an 80% failure rate. Recently, e-cigarettes are being promoted as a way to stop smoking, and this is discussed in detail below.

Success rate

So, what's the success rate of the Symonds Method?

In my experience, 80% of people stop smoking after coming to see me once and a further 10% of the total stop after a second visit.

At this point I need to mention another important difference between what I offer and conventional stop-smoking methods.

Stopping smoking is the easy bit. The real challenge is *staying stopped* and how to do this is explained in detail later.

Once this is understood, it should be possible for all smokers easily to return to the normal state of being non-smokers again.

I ask all patients who come to see me for help in quitting smoking to agree that in the unlikely event they don't happily stop after the first session they will come back as many times as necessary (free of additional charge).

Of the hundreds of smokers I've treated, most stop after one visit, a few come twice and in rare instances they come more than that.

You may then ask, what about those who don't come back but are still smoking?

This question raises an interesting point.

Suppose someone with my help quits for a year, and the next day, quite voluntarily, starts smoking again. Does this mean the Symonds Method has failed?

No, it means the smoker has *changed his or her mind* about wanting to quit and has decided to be a smoker once more.

I know from my experience of treating hundreds of smokers that if you successfully quit for a time there may be situations where you might be tempted to start again.

If someone unthinkingly gives way to such temptation, this represents a lapse by the smoker – not a failure of my method.

I do from time to time see smokers I've previously treated who are in this situation. There's always a reason why it's happened and if they come back for another session we use this in a constructive way to avoid it in the future.

Different from other methods

The Symonds Method can't really be compared with other methods of stopping smoking that claim a certain percentage of successes.

It's an *entirely new way of looking at smoking* that, once it's understood (very easy), should enable you to remain smoke-free for the rest of your life.

Is there a money-back guarantee?

Monkey-back guarantee if you don't stop smoking with the Symonds Method

Please read the caption carefully!

This is not meant as a joke – it's what will happen if you don't stop smoking.

You want to get rid of the Nicotine Monkey once and for all, but in a sense you quite like him being there!

Nonetheless, the best way to defeat him is not through fear, not through being bullied by anti-smoking activists, not through willpower (this is *really* hard) – but through *understanding*.

This will enable you to develop a different attitude to smoking so that you can get the Nicotine Monkey off your back permanently and without a struggle.

In other words, you'll have no difficulty in not smoking if you don't want to do it anymore!

About the picture

The wonderful picture shown opposite, 'Nicotine Monkey on the Back' by Don Ivan Punchatz, graphically shows the situation smokers are in.

The expression 'monkey on the back' in general means a serious problem or, more particularly, it refers to drug addiction.

The young man in the picture is smoking a cigarette – and there are plenty more where that came from!

He looks rather doubtful, as well he might, as he turns towards the Nicotine Monkey who has a cigarette pack in one paw and two more held in his tail.

The Monkey's claws are digging in, he has an evil grin and horrid orange eyes which reflect the seductive golden colour of his tobacco leaf wings.

If you keep this image in mind as representing your smoking problem, you will learn how the Symonds Method can help you get the Nicotine Monkey off your back for good.

There's no magic wand to stopping smoking but I like to think the Symonds Method is the nearest thing to it. It's designed to help you gain knowledge and understanding of two essential things:

The real reason you smoke now, and
Why it seems so difficult to stop.

To put it another way, the object of the Symonds Method – which you should find easy and interesting to follow – is that at the end of it you won't want to smoke anymore!

The most important quitting resource of all

All the conventional approaches to quitting smoking – nicotine gum or patches, e-cigarettes, prescription drugs, counselling by stop-smoking clinics and gimmicks like hypnosis – rely on something outside the smoker to assist or even take over the task for you.

They have limited effectiveness and, as you will soon see, are all unnecessary and even counterproductive.

There's only one method or way of quitting that really matters: YOURSELF.

You already have in you – in your intelligence and ability to think – the means of successful quitting.

And the key that will enable you to unlock this wonderful resource is *understanding*.

4 Steps

The purpose of this book is to reproduce in written form what takes place in my face-to-face quit-smoking sessions that have proven so successful with hundreds of individual smokers.

This unique approach is interactive and consists of four steps. These are colour-coded to key in with the corresponding parts of the text.

QUESTIONS. This is an information-gathering exercise to get a clear idea about why you started smoking and your current thinking about it.

UNDERSTANDING. You'll be shown how the answers to the questions will enable you to demonstrate to yourself the real reason you continue to smoke.

INSTRUCTION. Keeping this understanding in mind, you'll be able to take the one simple step to stop smoking easily and permanently.

TIME TO START your smoke-free life. The above three steps will show you why the best time to quit is *right now*.

How to use the Symonds Method

Although you might succeed in quitting smoking just by reading through the book, to get the best out of it, proceed as follows.

For the QUESTIONS part below, please write down your answers in the spaces provided. If there isn't enough room (or if you prefer anyway), use a separate sheet of paper.

There are no right or wrong answers. Whatever you can think of is part of your experience of smoking and you'll see the importance of this as we progress.

Questions

1. Your smoking history

a. How old were you when you smoked your first cigarette?

Answer:

b. Why did you smoke that first cigarette?

Answer:

c. What was it like, or what effect did it have on you?

Answer:

d. How long after your first cigarette was it until you were smoking regularly, that is, at least several cigarettes daily or on most days?

Answer:

e. How many per day did you smoke when you first became a regular smoker?

Answer:

f. How many per day do you smoke now?

Answer:

2. Why do you smoke now? What does it do for you or what do you get out of it?

Answer:

3. Why do you want to stop smoking?

Please make a list:

4. What do you actually feel when you feel like having a cigarette?

Answer:

Question 4 is not so simple as it may seem, but it's the key to successful quitting! Try to write down as much as you can. If you can't think of anything, that's fine too, and if this applies in your case it's significant of itself.

It may help to imagine a scenario where you want to smoke but aren't allowed to, such as being longer than expected on a flight or in a non-smoking meeting, or imagine you've run out of cigarettes.

Many smokers will say they don't know what this would be like because they've never been in such a situation!

Nonetheless, it's very important to try to remember *what you actually feel when you feel like you want a cigarette.*

You might even try an experiment: deliberately avoid smoking for a few hours (or longer if possible), and monitor how you feel as the time goes by.

Every hour write down exactly what you're feeling (if anything) and rate it on a scale of how bad (or mild) it is.

You might use a scale such as this:

0 – Don't notice anything
1 – Mild discomfort, easy to ignore
2 – Moderate discomfort, difficult to ignore
3 – Very troublesome symptoms
4 – Feel like jumping out of the window!

It's important that you have written down your answers to the above questions before proceeding.

Understanding

This step is much the longest and will repay careful reading. Many people say they find it interesting and even enjoyable to follow.

You'll have your answers to the various questions written down.

Now we'll compare them with my comments.

Typical Answers

1. Your smoking history

a. How old were you when you smoked your first cigarette?

Most people start in their teens.

b. Why did you smoke that first cigarette?

The usual reason is because friends or parents were smokers, or it may have been just 'the thing to do'. Perhaps it was because you wanted to feel grown-up or you tried smoking out of curiosity. Rebelliousness may have come into it: you weren't allowed to smoke so of course you wanted to try.

c. What was it like, or what effect did it have on you?

Typically, people say it was not pleasant: it caused dizziness or they felt sick and it made them cough. If, however, you thought it was enjoyable, that's all right.

d. How long after your first cigarette was it until you were smoking regularly, that is, at least several cigarettes daily or on most days?

Usually, it was only a short time – maybe a few months or occasionally a few years. Some people were regular smokers straight away after their first cigarette.

e. How many per day did you smoke when you first became a regular smoker?

It may have been five to ten per day.

f. How many per day do you smoke now?

Most smokers, as time goes by, find the number of cigarettes smoked daily increases.

You'll soon see how to use this information. In the meantime we should note that nearly all smokers' smoking histories are remarkably similar.

2. Why do you smoke now?

This is very important!

To put it another way: what does smoking do for you, or what do you get out of it?

Most likely your answer is at least one of the following:

a. I don't know
b. I'm only a social smoker / I only smoke with a drink
c. Enjoyment, especially with a drink/coffee/after a meal
d. Stress relief
e. Helps me take a break
f. Habit
g. Social situations
h. My friends and/or co-workers smoke
i. Helps concentration
j. Weight control
k. Boredom
l. Something to do with my hands
m. Nicotine addiction
n. It takes away the desire for a cigarette – until I want the next one!

We'll now look at each of these in detail

a. I don't know

    This is a common answer. It would indicate that for
    many people smoking has no obvious point or benefit.

b. I'm only a social smoker / I only smoke with a drink

    These are what I call the *imonly* and *ionly* smokers,
    respectively.

    (We need not be concerned with the very small
    minority of people who only smoke occasionally, say,
    once a week or on special occasions – though they
    too should stop because even one cigarette harms
    your health. The vast majority of people who smoke
    at all, do it repeatedly every day, and they may refer
    to themselves as regular or confirmed smokers.)

    It makes not the slightest difference whether you're an
    imonly or an *ionly* or just an ordinary smoker: a smoker
    is a smoker. There are *only* two things you can be with
    regard to smoking: either you smoke – or you don't.

    The *ionly* or *imonly* kind of response is given, perhaps
    unthinkingly, an excuse or justification for smoking.

c. Enjoyment, especially with a drink or coffee or after a meal

    This is also a common answer.

    But think about it. Do you see a vision of heaven or
    experience some real pleasure every time you light up?

Do you actually smoke twenty cigarettes a day (or however many it is) because you *enjoy* it?

Look at people smoking. Do they look *happy*? Do they look as if they're *enjoying* themselves?

Observe people in a public smoking area or outside an office building. They're taking a few minutes' break, being forced to interrupt what they were doing before, to stand in the open, rain or shine, to top up their nicotine levels!

Doing this is *boring*. Often they're looking at their phones to help pass the time while they get through the cigarette. Again, one may ask, do smokers smoke because they enjoy it?

Maybe, then, if you say smoking is enjoyable, what you mean is the taste of cigarette smoke. But what is it that you're supposed to be tasting? Do you mean the taste of the tobacco fumes in your mouth?

If so, is this so wonderful that you feel you have to experience it twenty times a day, every day? (If you smoke more or fewer than twenty cigarettes a day, this is the number that applies.)

Or maybe you mean the smell. Then why not let the lit cigarette smoulder like an incense stick?

Why do you feel you have to *inhale the fumes* to experience the smell? Do you go into a room full of stale tobacco smoke, take a lungful and exclaim, *What a charming aroma!?*

Or perhaps you mean the 'enjoyable' after-a-meal cigarette. You probably eat three meals a day, but you don't smoke only three cigarettes a day.

Why do you smoke all the others? In any case, it's very doubtful that these after-meal ones are actually enjoyable. More about this later.

So you see, if you talk about smoking being enjoyable, as if this explains the reason why you smoke, it doesn't make sense.

The reality is that smoking is *not* enjoyable – it's the opposite. It may *seem* to be enjoyable but this is an illusion – and there's a reason why it's an illusion which I'll explain later.

d. Stress relief

Other things being equal, who has more stress: the smoker or the non-smoker? Nicotine isn't a tranquilliser – it's a stimulant.

If you put nicotine into your body by smoking or by any other means your pulse and blood pressure will go up.

Smokers are in a stressed state all the time – although they may feel better immediately after having smoked a cigarette.

It's the temporary relief of this nicotine-induced stress by another dose of the poison nicotine that creates the illusion that smoking calms you down.

In reality, smoking does not and cannot help relieve the stress of life's normal difficulties and disappointments.

e. Helps me take a break

Why can't you take a break without a cigarette? And how is it you need so many breaks anyway?

More likely, rather than smoking helping you to take a break, *you take a break in order to smoke.* Is this not true?

f. Habit

Habit is not the reason you smoke.

If it were so, you could easily give it up or change it. This is one of the many excuses smokers use because they don't really understand why they smoke.

Or they may just say 'habit' when asked why they smoke because it's a common idea and they haven't given it much thought.

g. Social situations

If anything, smoking interferes with social life since more and more people these days don't like to be around smokers.

The reality is that you probably feel less guilty about smoking if you're doing it with other smokers, that is, people who have also failed to quit.

And what about non-smokers? Don't they have a social life?

h. My friends/co-workers smoke

This is a common reason why people *start* smoking; it's not the reason they continue.

Will your smoking friends or co-workers disown you if you quit?

More likely, they will admire you and seek your advice on how they too can become non-smokers!

i. Helps concentration

Cigarettes may *seem* to help concentration but this is another illusion. I'll explain why in the section dealing with nicotine withdrawal.

Please think about why it seems difficult to concentrate without a cigarette? And how do non-smokers manage?

j.   Weight control

Smoking may have some effect in reducing appetite but there are plenty of fat people who smoke and many thin people who don't.

In any case, it's obviously a very dangerous way to control your weight.

Smokers sometimes say they're afraid to stop because they'll put on weight, but it's not the absence of smoking that makes people fat.

Also, strange as it may sound, since many smokers don't really *want* to quit (it's in the nature of addiction), they seize on the fear of weight gain as an excuse to carry on smoking.

It's similar to smokers saying they'll not be able to concentrate if they quit.

In reality, if you stop smoking, with your new-found sense of well-being and pride that you've overcome this dangerous addiction, you'll find it's not too difficult to use a little discipline to eat in a healthy way to control your weight.

Part of the fear of putting on weight if you stop smoking comes from the common idea, that if you force yourself not to smoke through willpower, you'll want to eat more, especially sweet things, as a *substitute* for smoking.

You don't *need* a substitute for smoking!

k. Boredom

A little thought will show this doesn't make sense.

If it were true, how long would smoking a cigarette relieve boredom for? Five minutes? And then what?

In any case, it's much more likely you're so busy there aren't enough hours in the day to do everything you want to do!

Also, as I mentioned in connection with the so-called enjoyable cigarette, smoking, rather than relieving boredom, *is itself boring*.

One of my patients put it like this:

Smoking occupies and wastes time.

l. Something to do with my hands

But you only use one hand to smoke! In any case, why not just hold the unlit cigarette, fiddle with a pen or clasp your hands in front of you?

And again, how do non-smokers manage?

m. Nicotine addiction

Correct! For the practical purpose of quitting smoking you need to understand this is the *only* reason you smoke.

n. It takes away the desire for a cigarette – until I want the next one!

This is the essence of nicotine addiction. We'll say more about it later.

In summary, for the practical purpose of quitting smoking, it's essential to understand that the only reason you smoke is drug addiction, the drug, of course, being nicotine.

How can I say this?

Because your smoking history, like any smoker's smoking history, shows it, as in this typical example:

You started smoking for no good reason – it was just because of peer pressure. The initial experience of smoking was not pleasant. But you were already hooked from the first cigarette – that's why you've continued to smoke. You learnt to get used to the unpleasant effects because you needed the nicotine. To start with you smoked about five cigarettes each day or on most days. Now, some years later, you're still smoking, every day, up to twenty cigarettes. You want to quit but find it too difficult.

This is addictive behaviour.

3. Why do you want to stop smoking now?

If you had difficulty finding reasons *for* smoking, probably you had no hesitation in thinking of a number of important reasons for quitting.

Compare your list with the following:

Health – worry about cancer and heart disease; lack of physical fitness.

Money – it's a terrible waste! Think what you could spend it on instead.

Stinks – self-evident.

Slavery – many people hate being dependent on tobacco.

Inconvenience – it's becoming more and more difficult to find a place outside your home where you're allowed to smoke.

Social disapproval – increasing.

Bad example to children – if you're a smoker who has children you don't want them to start.

Makes you look older – I find it remarkable that when my patients stop smoking and if I see them a week later their appearance has improved: they're usually bright-eyed, with a clearer complexion and generally seem younger, healthier and more relaxed. Smokers do have a certain look about them: the 'smoker's face' – lines and bags. This is quite different from the normal changes in a non-smoker's face as he or she ages.

(There's an amusing story about the Jazz musician George Melly who once asked Mick Jagger why his face was so wrinkled. 'Those aren't wrinkles,' said Mick, 'they're laughter lines.' Melly replied, 'Nothing's *that* funny.' Mick Jagger, as is well known, is a heavy smoker.)

Higher life insurance premiums – smokers are invariably charged more for life or health insurance.

All of the above

It's important to keep in mind your reasons for wanting to quit as we progress through the Symonds Method.

Summary of what we've learnt so far

Smokers often seem to be on the verge of understanding what's really going on; they just need a little help to put it all together.

Why is it that many smokers say 'I don't know' when they're asked why they smoke?

The fact that they often find it difficult to come up with reasons for smoking is significant.

Isn't it curious that they may smoke many cigarettes every day but don't seem to know why?

Smoking is full of contradictions and paradoxes of this sort. In my experience, quite a few smokers when asked why they smoke, say things like these:

- I enjoy smoking – but it's not really enjoyable
- It relaxes me – but I know it doesn't
- It tastes nice – but actually it tastes awful
- It helps me concentrate – but I know that's not true

On the other hand, when smokers are asked why they want to quit, usually they have no hesitation in giving a list of sound reasons.

It's worth repeating the most important of them, and I've added comments to the first two:

- Health. *Good health is beyond price*
- Money. *Work out what you spend, that is, waste, on smoking in six months or a year; it may surprise you*
- Bad example to children
- Inconvenience
- Hate being a slave to tobacco
- Higher life insurance premiums

Now, if we compare, on the one hand, the reasons smokers typically give for smoking (if they can think of any), and on the other hand, the extremely important motives they have for wanting to quit, it's unarguable that the only sensible thing to do is just to quit!

So why don't they?

The answer is that smoking is not much to do with logic but everything to do with nicotine addiction. This will be explained soon.

Crucial part of the 'Understanding' step

4. What do you actually feel when you feel like having a cigarette?

The answer to this question is the key to successful quitting.

It's important that you have written down your answer before reading further.

It will probably include one or more of the following:

- Nothing
- Don't know
- I feel like I want a cigarette
- Anxious
- Irritable or short-tempered
- Distracted or have difficulty in concentrating
- Feel as if something is missing

If you have used the suggested scoring system it's unlikely you would have recorded anything more than a '2' in terms of severity.

Nearly all other methods of smoking cessation trot out a long list of awful symptoms you may expect to suffer if you 'try' to quit, such as stomach upsets, depression, sleeping difficulties, cough, dizziness, headache and 'cravings'.

The good news is that these are largely untrue. The vast majority of people whom I've helped to quit smoking do not report such symptoms.

This is discussed in more detail next.

Case histories of actual patients

It's sometimes said there are as many reasons for smoking as there are smokers. This is wrong.

As already noted, all smokers smoke for the same, one reason: nicotine addiction. This is shown by the fact that all smokers' smoking histories are remarkable similar.

Here are some typical case histories taken at random from the last one hundred smokers I've treated recently.

Ms T B, age 25

Started smoking aged 16 because her parents and friends smoked.

Effects of first cigarette: 'Awful, really bad, felt quite sick.' Regular smoker a few months later, initially 10 per day. Now smokes 10-12 per day.

Perceived benefits of smoking: Two or three for relaxation, the rest are from habit. It relaxes her, especially after a day at work. 'It's part of my personality.'

Reasons for wanting to quit: Health. Doesn't want to smoke forever. 'It's pointless to smoke.'

What happens if she doesn't smoke: feels anxious (said after much hesitation).

<u>Mr O Y, age 38</u>

Started aged 13 from peer pressure – it seemed cool and rebellious.

Effects of first cigarette: Not that pleasant. Felt ill the next day.

Regular smoker by age 17 when he smoked up to 10 per day. Now smokes 20 per day.

Reasons for smoking: Doesn't know. 'I need to smoke but this is questionable. Helps me to concentrate and take a 5 minute break, a chance to reflect. Body is used to it as a stimulant. Never satisfied with one cigarette but I want to be content without a cigarette.'

Reasons for wanting to quit: Health and money. 'I want to be happy in a room without having to smoke.'

What happens if he doesn't smoke: Feels anxious and frustrated but after a while it subsides.

Mr H L, age 39

Started smoking aged 14 because friend introduced him to it.

Effects of first cigarette: Horrible, felt dizzy, had to lie down. Was spaced out.

Regular smoker 2 months later at 10 - 15 per day. He tried to smoke more but was limited by unpleasant effects.

Now smokes 20 - 30 per day.

Reasons for smoking: 'Because of fear of not being allowed to smoke, especially when getting near to a non-smoking environment.' [Note: this is a very perceptive comment.]

Likes cigarette with coffee and a glass of water. Feels comfortable when he smokes. For many cigarettes he doesn't know what the trigger is. He wakes up and wants to smoke. It fulfills a need which is repeated 10 minutes to 2-3 hours later.

Reasons for wanting to quit: Health, and to prove to himself that he can stop.

What happens if he doesn't smoke: Feels nervous, anxious; it is an unpleasant feeling.

Mr B L, age 41

Started smoking aged 14 to feel grown up.

Effects of first cigarette: 'Not very pleasant at all.' Regular smoker at 17 when he smoked 8 - 10 per day because it seemed 'cool'.

Now smokes 20 per day and in the last week has smoked 40 per day due to impending cessation [with Dr Symonds]!

Smokes to take a break, with a drink, as a routine, for social reasons – the camaraderie; 'It keeps me from wanting another cigarette immediately'; nicotine addiction.

He added that the other cessation methods he's tried (pills, patches, gum) are all very stressful and produce side-effects.

If he doesn't smoke, experiences a near-panic feeling, fearfulness, unpleasantness.

Very likely you'll be able to see your own situation in these common smoking histories. The significant points in each case are the unimportant reasons for starting smoking, the unpleasant first effects, the unarguable reasons for wanting to quit and the statements of what happens if they didn't smoke.

After one session all these people stopped without difficulty and as far as I know are still non-smokers. The first-mentioned patient, *Ms T B*, sent me a follow-up message:

Dear Dr. Symonds,

I am happy to let you know, that I am still very much smoke free.

I can actually say that I enjoy being and seeing myself as a non-smoker and only experience very minimal cravings, which I can easily control.

Kind regards,

T.B.

Any smoker, with the right approach, can easily achieve this happy state!

Alleged difficulties of quitting

Why, then, are so many alleged unpleasant withdrawal symptoms quoted on the internet and in books as if they're gospel truths?

The main reason this happens is because of the way information on withdrawal symptoms is collected. Research in this area is usually done by questionnaires using use box-ticking methods.

Being confronted with lists of suggested answers, smokers may tick the boxes without giving them much thought:

> *The following is a list of nicotine withdrawal symptoms. Check all that apply to you: cravings, headaches, stomach pains, depression, nervousness, sleeping difficulties, etc.*

But what happens if one asks open-ended questions?

One hundred smokers

I surveyed the records of the last one hundred patients I saw for smoking cessation in face-to-face sessions. These records, like the examples quoted above, contain near-verbatim accounts of what patients said when they were asked why they smoke.

In descending order of frequency these are the symptoms mentioned – most patients had more than one:

Anxiety	72%
Irritability	46%
Distraction	20%

Something missing	16%
Frustration	12%
Thinking about smoking a lot	8%
Panic	8%
Dry mouth/bad taste	3%
Light-headedness	3%
Headache	2%
Neck tightness	2%
Depression	2%
Sleepiness	2%
Others	1%

I've paraphrased some symptoms to avoid undue complexity. For example, if patients said they felt short-tempered I've put this under Irritability; difficulty in concentrating and insecurity, under Distraction; nervousness, restlessness and stress, under Anxiety.

Headache is frequently included in lists of alleged nicotine withdrawal symptoms. But as can be seen it was mentioned only twice among the hundred smokers.

In one case it referred to a feeling of tightness in the muscles at the back of the neck, so this could have been due to associated anxiety; it was stated as a specific symptom by only one person.

No one – not a single person out of a hundred – said they suffered stomach pains, constipation or diarrhoea, cough, sleeping difficulties or 'cravings' at any time after stopping smoking.

Is there perhaps some kind of conspiracy to make smokers think it will be so difficult and unpleasant to quit unaided that they'll need to use nicotine products or prescription drugs?

Smoking cessation using such 'aids' is a multibillion dollar industry.

Withdrawal symptoms and fear of quitting

You need to ask yourself: will such feelings as you do notice (if any) when you stop smoking ever become severe or intolerable? The answer is that *this will only happen if you think it will!*

Some smokers are *afraid* these feeling will become intolerable.

The reality is that for the vast majority of smokers they are mild. They may be noticeable but they are *not that bad*.

(If some who has recently quit smoking suffers more severe symptoms these should not be assumed to be due to the absence of smoking and medical advice should be sought.)

For the great majority of smokers when they become aware of the feeling that they 'need' another cigarette, what they actually experience is mild anxiety, irritability or distraction.

It should be noted that some smokers don't even have these. All they are aware of is the idea that they want a cigarette. It may from time to time be felt strongly, but it's *only an idea in the mind.*

It's also important to note what happens when you experience these feelings and then smoke another cigarette: *they go away – immediately!*

That's great, but how long do they go away for? They go away *until you want the next cigarette*, that is, after about forty minutes or an hour (or more or less, depending on the circumstances) – and then *they come back!*

But *why* do they come back?

The answer to this question is given in the next section; it's essential that you understand it.

Why you get nicotine withdrawal symptoms

As soon as you start inhaling tobacco smoke, nicotine is absorbed from your lungs into the bloodstream and is carried to your brain. This takes a few seconds.

You keep inhaling until you feel satisfied or comfortable. At this point you have achieved the level of nicotine that your brain has got used to – the Peak Nicotine Level.

It's important to realise that you're then in a *drugged state.*

Now, if you put nicotine into your bloodstream the body's cleansing mechanisms immediately go into action to get rid of it. It's eliminated mainly in the urine.

So the nicotine level in your bloodstream starts to fall as soon as you put out the cigarette you were smoking.

Until it reaches a critically low level – this may take forty minutes or an hour – you're in what I call your Comfort Zone.

As the level of nicotine starts to fall further, the Nicotine Monkey on your back whispers in your ear, very persuasively: *You need another cigarette!*

The reason the Nicotine Monkey does this is because nicotine withdrawal symptoms – those anxious irritable feelings or just the idea that you want another cigarette – start to make their unwelcome presence felt.

If circumstances allow, you don't usually wait until you're aware of these feelings, but you pre-empt them by smoking another cigarette, that is, you put another dose of the poison nicotine into your body.

This almost instantly relieves the withdrawal symptoms (or prevents them coming on) so you're back in your Comfort Zone and all seems well.

But all is not well.

What this cigarette does is to restore you to what, as a smoker, seems normal for you: *the temporary state in which you have relieved the discomfort of the withdrawal symptoms of nicotine.*

What we want to do, therefore, is to make this temporary state permanent.

That is to say, the object is to be in your Comfort Zone all the time. Of course, there are many things in life that cause irritation and anxiety but I'm not talking about the normal stressful events that anyone may go through.

All of us, smokers and non-smokers alike, have to deal as best we can with the inevitable problems and frustrations of ordinary life.

But smokers are in a *worse* situation, because they have all the time *in addition* another problem: nicotine withdrawal symptoms.

Smokers may or may not be aware of these symptoms coming on twenty times a day (or whatever is the number of cigarettes smoked daily), every day, because they have learnt to accept them as normal.

But what they actually experience (if anything), or are on the verge of experiencing, is *mild anxiety and irritability*.

However, when you feel better after having smoked a cigarette, the relief only lasts for about forty minutes or an hour; then the withdrawal symptoms come on again.

So you have another cigarette and the cycle repeats indefinitely – unless you do something about it.

It's vital to understand this process.

Please study the diagram below and I'll spell out the sequence again.

Diagram of what happens when you smoke

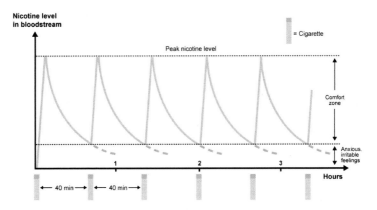

Smoke a cigarette: peak nicotine level quickly achieved; you immediately feel better as the anxious irritable feelings are relieved. Nicotine level starts to fall.

Next forty minutes (approx): in Comfort Zone and feel all right. Nicotine level is falling.

Critical nicotine level reached (lower horizontal dotted line in diagram): klaxon sounds, warning light flashes, Nicotine Monkey digs his claws in and whispers urgently in your ear: *Nicotine level critical. Smoke another cigarette NOW!*

You smoke another cigarette: nicotine level surges to peak, you immediately feel better...

Sequence repeats indefinitely...

Note: What I have written about what happens when the critical nicotine level is reached is exaggerated for clarity. All that actually happens is that the smoker may be aware of a mild uneasiness, a vague feeling that something is missing or he or she is starting to feel restless (antsy for Americans and Australians). Some smokers don't even feel that – they just have *an idea in their mind* that they feel like smoking another cigarette.

Why certain cigarettes seem enjoyable

After meals cigarettes

Since you don't normally smoke when you're eating, by the end of a meal there will be a slightly longer than usual gap between the last cigarette and the next one.

This means that the withdrawal symptoms will be felt a little more intensely, insofar as you are aware of them at all, so their relief will be perceived slightly more strongly as well.

This feels enjoyable in the same sense as when you stop banging your head against the wall!

Smoking is not inherently enjoyable; it merely relieves the temporary mildly uncomfortable withdrawal feelings, and this is perceived as enjoyable.

It's an illusion, not reality.

How much nicer would it be not to have the discomfort in the first place! Yet this discomfort-free state is what non-smokers enjoy all the time, other things being equal.

Stress-relieving cigarettes

The apparent relief of stress with smoking is explained similarly.

Smoking is not a tranquilliser.

It's impossible for smoking to help the normal troubles of ordinary life. It *seems* to help because, as already mentioned, whatever problem you have to deal with, you have in addition to cope with nicotine withdrawal symptoms.

So, when you have some stress or difficulty and you smoke a cigarette and feel better, you are *merely relieving the stress that is caused by nicotine withdrawal;* the underlying situation is obviously unchanged.

Apart from smoking being of no help in dealing with stress, it actually makes it worse.

We have noted that nicotine is a stimulant: it puts your heart rate up and increases your blood pressure and, if you're not used to it, may stimulate you to the point of dizziness or nausea.

Thus, *if you smoke twenty cigarettes a day, you're in a mildly stressed state twenty times a day.*

Let me put this another way – it's vital that you understand it:

Smokers are either in a drugged state when they've just smoked, or they're suffering drug (nicotine) withdrawal symptoms when they feel the need for the next cigarette.

Instruction

The obvious – indeed, the only – way to stop the vicious cycle of nicotine withdrawal symptoms followed by short-lived relief through smoking another cigarette followed by withdrawal symptoms is:

STOP PUTTING NICOTINE INTO YOUR BODY!

Unless you do this, you will remain in the unfortunate situation where

each cigarette you smoke will create the need for the next one.

You must keep it clearly in mind that if you have that next cigarette, inevitably and necessarily, you will want another one!

But if you stop putting nicotine into your body – just like that – what about withdrawal symptoms?

It's understandable to be concerned about this. But we've already noted that the withdrawal symptoms are nothing more than mild anxiety, irritability or distraction. There's no actual pain.

You might *be afraid* these symptoms will become severe or intolerable. This is what many people believe: that you'll be chewing the wall and climbing the carpet. (Or is it the other way round?)

There are even clichés about this: 'My nerves will be shot to pieces' or 'I'll be hell to live with'; and unkind jokes: 'Oh, the pangs, the pangs!'

The reality is: THIS IS NOT TRUE!

It's never been known in the history of the world that these feeling will become intolerable so that you'll want to jump out of the window if you can't have another cigarette!

It's essential to develop a new attitude based on the reality of smoking, and to put aside all the misinformation and illusions which nearly everybody believes.

If you do this you'll realise

THERE IS NOTHING TO GIVE UP EXCEPT THE FEAR OF NOT SMOKING

And by keeping this in mind you'll be able to replace the fear of not smoking with the truth that

IT'S WONDERFUL TO BE A NON-SMOKER!

You may also be afraid you'll lose something important: the enjoyable cigarette or the helpful cigarette, or both.

It cannot be repeated too often: these ideas are illusions.

Smoking is not enjoyable – it's horrible. Nor is it helpful in any way, for example as a tranquilliser – it winds you up rather than calms you down. Nor is it an aid to concentration – it makes concentration more difficult.

The reality is that if you stop smoking, or in other words, if you stop putting the poison nicotine into your body, you will achieve two wonderful goals:

1) You will no longer be in a drugged state with nicotine all the time

2) You will no longer suffer drug withdrawal symptoms

Now let's think about what may happen if you haven't smoked for a while and you become aware of the mild anxious irritable feelings.

If you don't have another cigarette what will happen to these feelings?

Check all that apply:

☐ They will become intolerable
☐ They will be with me forever
☐ I will want to jump out of the window
☐ They will go away

You ticked the last box, did you not?

That's right: they will go away!

They will go away and never come back – *unless you put more nicotine into your body* – which, of course, from now on you will never want to do again.

How long will it take for these feelings to go away permanently?

It usually takes three or four days, exceptionally up to ten days.

After about four days there will be no detectable nicotine left in your body, so how can you experience withdrawal symptoms from something that is already completely withdrawn?

Many people, with the right frame of mind based on knowledge of the reality of smoking, don't experience *any* withdrawal symptoms because they're so delighted with the idea they can stop straight away and permanently just by having the right attitude.

If you do become aware of withdrawal symptoms, you can tell yourself:

> *This is what it feels like as the last vestige of the poison nicotine is being cleansed from my body. This is marvelous! Soon these artificially caused slightly unpleasant feelings will be gone for good.*

If from time to time in the next few days you do become aware of the anxious irritable feelings, DON'T LET THEM BOTHER YOU – JUST CONTINUE WITH YOUR USUAL ACTIVITIES.

You must be absolutely clear that if you do smoke another cigarette to get rid of these feelings, it's guaranteed they will come back in full force after about forty minutes.

So, do you want to experience these feelings for a few days (if at all) or repeatedly, every day for the rest of your life?

ANOTHER KEY TO SUCCESSFUL SMOKING CESSATION IS IN THE WORD 'TEMPTATION'

If you feel tempted to smoke you are thinking about it in the old, wrong way.

No one in their right mind would ever be tempted to inhale tobacco smoke.

Therefore, please adjust your attitude!

One reason for giving in to the temptation to smoke is to do with the nature of addiction: illogical though it is, you might not really want to quit.

We can picture this as the horrid Nicotine Monkey on your back who doesn't want to let go. He's very clever in the deceitful way he tries to manipulate you. There he is, digging his claws in and whispering in your ear:

Go on, have another one. You need it. You deserve it. Think of all the stress you have – you'll be able to cope better with a smoke – everyone knows that! Anyway, now's not the right time to quit – wait till you feel ready. Have just one more cigarette to prove to yourself you can give up anytime you want!

This is when you need to say to the Nicotine Monkey:

Will you please be quiet and go away!

or words to that effect.

He may then start to get a bit desperate as he digs his claws in deeper and says things like:

You're not going to let those nicotine nazis, the nanny state, those anti-smoking do-gooders tell you what to do! You're not going to be pushed around by that lot! Why shouldn't you have a smoke if you jolly well want to?!

Your reply:

I said will you please be quiet and go away. I don't need you anymore!

If you do this, something wonderful will happen: the Nicotine Monkey's claws will relax and his voice will get fainter.

He'll realise he's wasting his time with you. Because you now understand that everything he's been telling is lies.

So remind yourself of the truth:

Smoking

- produces a drugged state
- is not enjoyable
- is not relaxing
- does not relieve stress
- does not help concentration
- is utterly and completely pointless

Now ask yourself whether it's really so difficult to replace the fear of not smoking with the truth that it's great to be a non-smoker!

Time to Start Your Smoke-Free Life

Quitting smoking, as I have indicated, is largely a problem of how you think about it.

Therefore, you need to acquire a new attitude to smoking. You should have been able to do this by following the previous steps of the Symonds Method. Let me repeat the three main points:

1. You smoked only because of nicotine addiction
2. The reason it seemed difficult to stop was because of nicotine withdrawal symptoms
3. Such withdrawal symptoms as you do experience are not that bad

I have deliberately put the first two sentences in the past tense.

The question, then, for the Time to Start, is this: are you going to do it?

Are you *right now* going to begin enjoying the rest of your life without smoking or using any kind of nicotine product ever again?

You may be thinking it can't be that simple. But the reality is that it *is* that simple!

This worry, if you have it, arises from a faint echo of the Nicotine Monkey's talk, picking up on the idea you used to have that you didn't really want to stop.

You need to be on your guard against such thoughts entering your head. But note that the very fact you have doubts (if you do) is an indication of the old, wrong way of thinking about smoking.

Your last cigarette

Let's consider the last cigarette that you will ever smoke (or did ever smoke) in your life.

Your attitude towards and feelings about this cigarette are of the highest importance.

Other stop smoking methods tend to view this final cigarette as if you're saying goodbye to an old and dear friend. It's part of the problem of 'preparing' to quit and setting a 'quit date'.

Similarly, you might want to finish the pack so as not to 'waste' any of the cigarettes you've already bought – but if you do smoke them it's the cigarettes that will waste you!

Many smokers believe cigarettes are enjoyable or helpful in some way, but for the sake of their health and for other good reasons such as saving money, they know it's only sensible to say goodbye to smoking.

If you approach quitting in this way, with regrets and doubts, it's likely you'll also experience the dreaded 'urges' or 'cravings' to smoke again and, worst of all, you'll suffer awful withdrawal symptoms!

I've already said a lot about the common idea that this is what you'll have to endure when you give up smoking, but here I'll use only three words: Nonsense! Rubbish! Untrue!

You aren't going to say Goodbye to cigarettes.

You're going to say *Good riddance!*

Cigarettes are NOT your friend, your crutch, your pleasure, your stress-reliever, your aid to concentration or enhancer of enjoyment of food or drink.

(If you think they are please re-read the section 'Why do you smoke now?')

Therefore, it's of the greatest importance that you stop smoking *right now*. Don't put it off till the 'right time' – it will never be the right time.

And don't think of putting it off till the happy day when you have less stress – as a smoker you are always stressed.

If you have a half-finished pack of cigarettes, throwing it into the dustbin (trash can) is an important symbolic – indeed liberating – act: you don't *need* cigarettes anymore!

How Mark Twain gave up smoking

Mark Twain famously said:

> *Giving up smoking is the easiest thing in the world. I know because I've done it thousands of times.*

Every time a smoker stubs out a cigarette they have given up smoking – until they want the next one. This is because all they achieve by smoking is *merely the temporary relief of the urge to smoke.*

Let me remind you: there are two stages in smoking cessation.

One is stopping; the other is staying stopped.

The art of staying stopped, therefore, is to know what to do if you feel tempted to smoke again.

We've already discussed this but I would like to share with you the following ideas that I have found helpful for those smokers who may still have difficulty.

As always, understanding is the key to the problem.

Let's consider what happens as time goes by after you've smoked your last cigarette.

What happens after you stop smoking

Four hours

What's likely to happen in the first four (or a few) hours after your last cigarette?

The short answer is – nothing. Or you'll probably be feeling excited at the prospect of stopping smoking easily.

Four days

Many of my patients, having gained a proper understanding of why they used to smoke, find it's easy to ignore such desires as they may have to smoke again in the next few days.

If the idea that you want a cigarette is more persistent, ask yourself what it amounts to.

The answer is that it's nothing worse than mild anxiety or a vague feeling that something is missing. *These are only ideas in your mind.*

There is no cause for worry or alarm.

Just take note that this is how you feel and remind yourself that it's due to the nicotine being cleansed from your body.

Be happy about it!

Don't worry that these feelings may become severe or intolerable – they won't. You can picture this as the Nicotine Monkey, with increasing desperation, trying to make you smoke again.

But now you know what to say to him!

It's most important simply to carry on with whatever you were doing when you became aware of the idea that you 'wanted a cigarette'.

You don't need to *do* anything about it – such as eating a healthy snack, drinking a glass of water, taking deep breaths or distracting yourself – this is giving it far too much importance!

The feeling or idea that you want a cigarette will just go away naturally.

Four months

Some of the same feelings may recur from time to time in the next few months after your last cigarette and you can deal with them in the same way.

As time goes by you will have longer and longer periods without thinking about smoking and eventually you will probably forget about it altogether.

Other methods of smoking cessation will tell you to be aware of 'triggers' and avoid them if possible.

This is pointless and unnecessary.

You didn't smoke in the past because of triggers, but as I hardly need remind you, because of nicotine withdrawal symptoms.

If one of the so-called triggers was having a cup of coffee, what are you supposed to do – give up coffee?

If you carry on normally (apart from smoking, of course) you may well find you're not drinking so much coffee as you used to, and this is probably better for your health.

(Why is it that many smokers drink rather a lot of coffee? Because coffee to some extent disguises the unpleasant taste of cigarette smoke and thereby makes it easier for smokers to get their next nicotine fix when they suck poison-laden fumes into their lungs!)

The fact that you've stopped smoking is no reason of itself to change anything else in your life.

Forever!

This is the happy state you were in before you started smoking and that non-smokers are in all the time, other things being equal.

You're infinitely better off – can there be ever the slightest doubt about it? – as a non-smoker.

Why, then, do some smokers even years after quitting still yearn for a cigarette?

It's because they've quit through willpower and are forcing themselves not to smoke even though they think they need or would enjoy a cigarette under certain circumstances.

This is due to misperceptions about smoking. It's explained above in the sections dealing with the so-called enjoyable or stress-relieving cigarettes.

Coping with difficulties without smoking

Some people who have recently stopped smoking find (or think they find) they can't cope with the normal difficulties and stresses of everyday life; they blame this on the absence of cigarettes and use it as an excuse to start smoking again.

For example, if you've had an argument with someone or your computer has crashed, you would feel annoyed and unhappy.

In your smoking days the first thing you would probably do would be to reach for a cigarette, if you weren't already smoking one, because it *seemed* to make you feel better. Why was this?

You'll remember it's because, as a smoker, you were already in a slightly stressed state due to nicotine withdrawal; you had another cigarette and overall you felt better.

But you had merely relieved the mild stress caused by your nicotine addiction – the external situation was unchanged.

Therefore, you had the understandable but mistaken idea that smoking relieves stress. It doesn't.

It should help to keep in mind that, as a non-smoker, you'll be able to deal with the normal difficulties of life better than before because you won't have the stress of nicotine withdrawal all the time *in addition.*

Similarly, you'll be able to concentrate better on whatever you have to do because you won't suffer the almost constant distraction of mild nicotine withdrawal symptoms.

Smoke-free socialising

Another situation for which you need to be on your guard is meeting other smokers. This may happen in one of the diminishing number of public places where smoking is allowed or at a private party.

If you see someone smoking what will you think? How much fun that is? You wish you could do it without feeling guilty? That you can't enjoy the party without smoking?

Even if you're having a drink at home and no one else objects to cigarette smoke, are you really missing something if you don't smoke?

Previously, in social situations you may have felt more at ease by smoking – but only because immediately before you smoked you were not at ease due to nicotine withdrawal.

Smokers are never fully at ease, except they may think they are for a short time immediately after lighting up.

You will remember this is an illusion because you were then in a *drugged state*. So don't make the mistake of thinking smoking will make social situations more enjoyable – it won't.

Another ploy some smokers find helpful

Check from the internet what your life expectancy is according to your sex and country of origin, subtract your current age and multiply by the number of cigarettes you smoked daily.

For example, if you're a British man aged forty your life expectancy is 79.2 years, so you would expect to live another 39.2 years.

If you were a pack-a-day smoker you would smoke 20 x 365 x 39.2 = 286,160 cigarettes if you live the average life span. To smoke 286,160 cigarettes you would get through 14,308 packs.

A pack of Marlboro cigarettes measures 8.5 x 5 x 2 cm, a volume of 85 cubic cm. Therefore, 14,308 packs if piled up all together would occupy a space of about 1.2 cubic metres or 43 cubic feet.

Try to picture this in your mind's eye.

Now, the deal – the inescapable pact with the Nicotine Monkey – is that if you have just one more, you *must* smoke all the remaining 286,159 cigarettes in the rest of your life if you live for the average life-span, and if you go beyond this you'll have to smoke some more.

So what do you want to do? Smoke 286,000 cigarettes – or none?

As the Americans would say with their colourful use of English, this is a no-brainer. You can't have just one or the occasional one; it's all or nothing.

If you don't believe this, see what happens if you stop smoking for a week and then smoke just one cigarette.

It's almost inevitable you'll immediately be back on twenty a day (or whatever the number of cigarettes was that you smoked previously).

In any case, why would anyone in their right mind want even one occasional cigarette?

It represents the old, wrong way of thinking about smoking: that it's enjoyable or helpful somehow in relieving stress. *These ideas are illusions.*

Nicotine Monkey still not wanting to let go?

In spite of all this some smokers find themselves still hesitating on the verge of starting their smoke-free life.

If you're in this position you need to understand the reason: you're trying to change the way of thinking about smoking that you had for many years in the short time you spent working through the Symonds Method.

It may take a little getting used to! You can also think of it as the Nicotine Monkey not wanting to let go of you – which is indeed in a pictorial form what's happening (if it does).

Therefore, you should once again politely – or not so politely (!) – tell him to *go away!*

You can visualise the horrid little fellow jumping down from your back and scuttling off till he's out of sight and hearing.

Here's another way of reinforcing your decision to quit smoking.

You could imagine (or actually do it if you're asked to) explaining the Symonds Method to another smoker. This will remind you of the principles of the method and help to fix them in your mind.

Desperate measure

A certain patient of mine thought of himself as a difficult case. We had been through my method three times, and although he said he understood it perfectly, he couldn't stop because of the illogical nature of smoking.

So he found an illogical solution.

He bought a duty-free pack of 200 cigarettes and put it, unopened, on his mantelpiece. There is has remained, unopened, and he has been a non-smoker for almost a year now.

Facing his fear enabled him to overcome it.

Non-smoker or ex-smoker?

I don't like the term ex-smoker. It sounds negative and implies you can never let go of your past in regard to smoking.

It's my hope that when you've worked through this e-book you'll never again think about smoking in the old way.

When non-smokers leave their home it would nonsensical for them to check that they have a cigarette pack in their pocket or handbag.

And probably the only time they would think about smoking is when they want to avoid it – such as by giving a wide berth to a smoker in the street.

The main difference, however, between someone who's never smoked and someone who's applied the Symonds Method of quitting, is that you need to be on your guard not to fall into the trap of thinking about smoking again in the old, wrong way!

If you can do this, from now on you will be able to

ENJOY THE EXHILARATION OF THE FREEDOM OF NOT SMOKING!

Appendix: Conventional Ways to Quit Smoking

Inherently discouraging

The approach of almost all other stop-smoking methods is inherently discouraging and makes it harder to succeed.

They will tell you that stopping smoking is going to be very difficult and will take a long time, it's like a journey, you have to prepare yourself for it and set a 'quit date' – as if you're going to take an exam or the driving test!

Then they make you even more worried by reminding you, as if you didn't know, of all the diseases you are at risk of getting through continuing to smoke: cancer, heart disease, lung disorders and other serious health problems.

It seems as if they're trying to make you quit smoking through fear – and this is doubtless the reason why cigarette packs these days are covered with horrible pictures.

As if all this isn't bad enough they also remind you that when you give up smoking you'll likely suffer unpleasant withdrawal symptoms that will go on for weeks or months. These are spelled out and typically include headaches, depression, stomach upsets, sleeping difficulties and 'cravings' (whatever that means).

Some stop-smoking clinics even offer to measure the carbon monoxide in your breath to underline the obvious fact that you're poisoning yourself with tobacco smoke!

All these conventional quitting methods imply you need willpower to quit (also known as cold turkey).

This is doubly unfortunate.

First, it's not true – the Symonds Method will have shown you why willpower is not needed.

Secondly, it again reinforces the mistaken idea that stopping smoking is terribly difficult.

You're almost defeated before you start.

Of course it's not all gloom and doom.

You'll also be reminded that after giving up smoking your risks of cancer and heart disease will decrease and your exercise ability will improve.

And you'll be able to smell the flowers. And you'll have more money to spend on other things.

All this is true but you already know it – that's why you want to quit!

Then, for practical help, what does it come down to?

As mentioned above, they use evidence-based treatments with an 80% failure rate, at best. What are these treatments?

As a smoker your problem is nicotine addiction. And the way they offer to treat it? With nicotine!

It's a bit like treating alcoholism with alcohol.

And if nicotine treatment doesn't work you'll probably be offered prescription drugs.

We'll shortly look at these in more detail, as well as consider some other conventional approaches to the smoking problem.

What can happen if you use willpower to stop smoking

The British National Health Service every year since 2012 has run a stop- smoking campaign called 'Stoptober' (because it started in the month of October).

This is a well-meant but gimmicky approach that uses humour (there's nothing funny about smoking) or trite sound bites to try to encourage smokers to quit.

One woman who tried the 2014 version posted these comments on Facebook:

> *wish u had more info as to the different things that stopping smoking can make u feel, ie, spaced out lack of concentration...lack of sleep at night, constant urge for loo, xtra peeing, eating more, bloating, wind. It would help more people if these subjects were covered on this official site, it's not always about the craving, I want to understand what's going on with my body and why its affected in this way...would love more info*

Two things stand out: the many physical symptoms she thinks are due to the absence of smoking and her desperate appeal for information.

I hope she saw a doctor to have these problems properly investigated.

What's wrong with nicotine replacement therapy (NRT)

First of all, the name is wrong.

Is nicotine going to be replaced *with* something, or is nicotine the replacement *for* something? The answer is neither.

NRT really means *cigarette* replacement.

It seems the idea is that you replace cigarettes with a different way of putting nicotine into your body – through the lining of the mouth with the chewing gum or through the skin with the patches.

Then after a few weeks you gradually wean yourself off the gum or patches and – Bingo! – you'll never want to smoke again.

If only it were that simple.

Since you keep putting nicotine into your body it keeps the addiction going.

Thus NRT in practice is a form of nicotine *maintenance*. Where's the logic in that?

Secondly, offering NRT to smokers reinforces the widely held but wrong idea that quitting is terribly hard without some outside assistance – it's too difficult to do on your own.

Not only is this approach discouraging, but it disempowers and even infantilises smokers.

Thirdly, since many (if not all) smokers *don't really want to quit,* medicinal nicotine can provide an inbuilt excuse for failure.

Smokers can say, 'I tried NRT – and *it* didn't work!' They can then feel slightly better about continuing to smoke which, even if they don't admit it, in a sense they're quite happy to do.

Fourthly, even if you do manage to stop with the hindrance of NRT, when you spit out the last piece of gum or tear off the last skin patch, what's to stop you from starting smoking again?

Finally, it assumes smoking is largely or entirely a physical addiction, but in reality it's mainly a problem of how you think about it.

What's wrong with e-cigarettes

E-cigarettes are becoming popular as an allegedly much safer way of taking nicotine into your body – and thereby continuing to be addicted.

(These devices don't burn tobacco but heat liquid nicotine together with propylene glycol, glycerol and flavourings to create a vapour which you can suck into your lungs. This is known as vaping and people who do it are called vapers. Depending on the brand the vapour may also contain traces of heavy metals and other chemicals which might be harmful over the long term.)

But if people enjoy using e-cigarettes and if they're much less harmful than smoking, what's wrong with that?

This is what's wrong:

First of all, as I said earlier, if you wish to stop smoking you presumably wish to get the Nicotine Monkey off your back once and for all. This obviously means you completely stop putting nicotine into your body – by any means.

Secondly, is vaping really enjoyable?

If you're a vaper, take half-a-dozen deep sucks on your e-cig device and then ask yourself what is so wonderful about it. As has been shown in the discussion about cigarettes, the so-called enjoyment of nicotine is an illusion.

Therefore, there's no good reason to use e-cigarettes.

Thirdly, although vaping appears to be much safer than smoking, we don't yet know that it's safe.

There are many potentially harmful chemicals in the vapour, albeit in very small amounts, but if you vape many times a day every day for years on end, as vapers typically do, nobody yet knows what will happen.

I predict it won't do your health any good and it could cause serious problems.

Fourthly, some people use e-cigarettes as a way of cutting down the number of cigarettes they smoke, so they use both. Smoking fewer cigarettes, however, does very little to protect your health compared with stopping completely.

Apart from this, many smokers give up normal cigarettes and switch to e-cigarettes as a long-term alternative.

They don't seem to understand that you don't need an alternative – long term or otherwise – to cigarettes. It's pointless, unnecessary and potentially harmful to put nicotine in any form into your body.

Why take the risk?

What's wrong with stop-smoking medicines

So-called stop-smoking medicines are prescription drugs which may be offered instead of, or even in addition to, nicotine products.

Two are in common use: bupropion (Zyban) and varenicline (Champix, Chantix).

It's not known exactly how they work, if they do, but they may have some effect in reducing so-called cravings for cigarettes.

But again, their use implies quitting is so difficult on your own that you need a drug to help you.

Furthermore, all drugs can have side-effects and these are no exception.

Perhaps because some doctors call smoking a chronic disease, which clearly it is not, this is the reason why they offer prescription drugs. (Chronic means long-continuing.)

Also, stop-smoking medicines, if they work at all, can only do this by themselves producing a drugged state in the brain.

Smokers are already in enough of a drugged state with nicotine, so it makes no sense to take an additional drug. Also, many people feel unwell while taking them and a serious (though rare) side-effect is suicidal thoughts.

Gimmicks

Hypnosis, acupuncture, laser treatment, etc., may work by suggestion but the fact that people have to go to the trouble and expense and spend time to undergo them, once again reinforces the wrong idea that quitting is too difficult to achieve on your own.

Further, they do nothing to help smokers understand why they smoke in the first place or how to avoid relapses.

Scare tactics

Horrible pictures on cigarette packs and other ways of reminding you about the health hazards of smoking assume you smoke because of ignorance of the risks.

Clearly, this is not the case.

Scare tactics have little effect or only make smokers feel guilty without doing anything to assist quitting.

The Symonds Method, other than the striking picture of the Nicotine Monkey, does not use scare tactics!

Summary

Conventional stop smoking methods –

* Often use fear to persuade you to quit
* Are inherently discouraging
* Are illogical in trying to treat nicotine addiction with nicotine or drugs

- Do very little or nothing to help you understand why you really smoke
- Do very little or nothing to help prevent relapses
- Have a low success rate

End

Readers are welcome to contact Dr Symonds by email with any questions or comments: info@nicotinemonkey.com

Numerous interesting blog posts can be found at www.nicotinemonkey.com

Made in the USA
Monee, IL
04 August 2020

37634123R00055

1 #5

THE ANGEL

a novel